BAKING IN A BOX,
COOKING ON A CAN

Explosives
Fire
Natural and Synthetic Poisons
What Makes a Lemon Sour?

BAKING IN A BOX, COOKING ON A CAN

by Gail Kay Haines

ILLUSTRATED BY MARGOT APPLE

William Morrow and Company
New York   1981

Printed in the United States of America.
1 2 3 4 5 6 7 8 9 10

Library of Congress Cataloging in Publication Data

Haines, Gail Kay.
    Baking in a box, cooking on a can.
    Includes index.
    Summary: Provides instructions for making and using outdoor cooking equipment such as a box oven, a paper bag cooker, and a toaster.
    1. Outdoor cookery—Juvenile cookery.   2. Kitchen utensils—Juvenile literature.   [1. Outdoor cookery.   2. Kitchen utensils]
I. Apple, Margot.   II. Title.
TX823.H26   641.5'78   80-26678
ISBN 0-688-00373-7
ISBN 0-688-00376-1 (lib. bdg.)

Contents

INTRODUCTION

Outdoor cooking is fun. But some people think it always means hot dogs black on one end and raw on the other, burned marshmallows, or camper stew that sticks to the bottom of the pot. Good outdoor cooks know better. They have learned ways to cook all their favorite foods out-of-doors and make them just as tasty as they are at home. In fact, food cooked outdoors usually tastes even better.

Suppose you want to bake a blueberry pie or a pizza. A cardboard box can be used as an oven. Or maybe you want to fix pancakes or fry a hamburger. A large tin can makes a handy stove top. If toasted cheese sandwiches sound good for lunch, you can turn two coat hangers into a toaster, and a paper bag can be used as a pan.

The equipment for all these different kinds of outdoor cooking is simple and easy to make. This book tells you how. You should be able to find everything you need around your home or neighborhood. All of the projects described are ones you can try for yourself, as long as an adult is watching. Use them to cook any of the recipes in this book or your own favorite foods. They are good for scout camping, family trips, or just cooking out in the backyard or on a city balcony.

But outdoor cooking is not as easy as turning on the stove or popping a pan of brownies into the oven. It takes practice and careful planning. It also takes extra caution, because cooking outdoors is more dangerous than cooking inside a kitchen. If you are a beginning outdoor cook, start with an easy recipe. If you are already a good camp cook, try something harder.

Whatever you do, don't skip the safety rules. It is important not to burn the food, but it is more important not to burn the cook.

Some Safety Basics for All Outdoor Cooking

1. Make or collect all your equipment before you start.

2. Choose a recipe and read it through. Be sure you have everything you need.

3. Have a bucket or pan of water ready to put out the fire.

4. Tie back long hair and roll up loose or floppy sleeves.

5. Have an adult who knows what you plan to do on hand. Even adult outdoor cooks have more fun and feel safer when someone else is around. Cooking is for sharing.

BAKING IN A BOX

Baking is a way of cooking that surrounds food with heat. The heat must be completely even, or some parts of the food will bake faster than others. In a kitchen, cooks bake food by placing it on a rack inside an oven heated by electricity or gas. Outdoors, a box oven heated with charcoal can do the same job. The next few pages will tell you how to make a box oven and use it safely.

A box oven can usually cook enough for a family or a patrol or den at one time. If you are cooking for more than eight people, you might want to use more than one oven. Your decision depends upon the recipe and whether you want to serve a small snack or a whole dinner.

The easiest foods to bake in a box oven are desserts. You can put them into the oven when the rest of the dinner is almost ready, and they will be done at just the right time. The hardest things to bake in a box oven are cookies and large, thin pizzas. Try them after you have baked some other things.

This book gives recipes for desserts and breads and main dishes and even vegetables. Start with one thing at a time. After you learn how easy it is to bake in a box, you may be ready to cook the whole meal.

Making a Box Oven

You will need:
a large cardboard box,
     18″ long × 12″ wide × 12″ high,
     or whatever size you can find that is
     large enough to fit around your pan,
     with room to spare on all sides
aluminum foil
a stapler (not absolutely necessary)
masking or Scotch tape

A box oven is made from an ordinary cardboard box, the kind you get from the grocery store. Cut off the flaps, so that your box has four straight sides and a bottom. The bottom of the box will be the top of the oven.

Line the inside of the box with long sheets

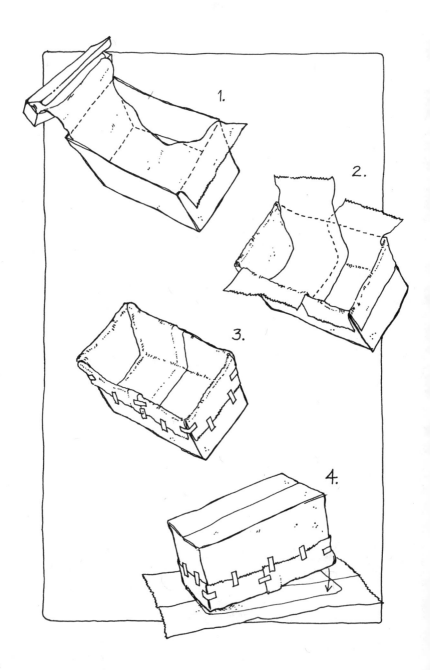

1.

2.

3.

4.

of foil, shiny side out. Make the first sheet long enough to cover both short sides and the bottom, with some foil hanging over each side.

If your box is wider than your foil, you may need two strips laid end-to-end. Just overlap them and use your fingers to poke the extra foil into the corners.

About 3 pieces of foil, overlapped, should be enough to cover the longer sides, going across the inside bottom each time and hanging extra foil over outside. It doesn't matter if the foil looks a little messy, but it is important to cover every part of the inside *completely* with foil.

Use tape to fasten the foil firmly to the *outside* of the box. Don't use tape inside. It will burn. If you overlap the foil enough and press it tightly into the corners, it may even stay in place all by itself. Turn the box upside down to check.

If the foil starts to come loose, use a stapler to fasten each strip to the side of the box. Make sure the sharp ends of the staples are inside the oven, so you won't scratch yourself on them. Staples that have to go through cardboard do not always close safely.

If you need to put any staples in the bottom of the box (the top of your oven), check the outside for sharp points poking through. If you find any, pad them with masking tape.

A box oven can be used over and over. So if you plan to bake lots of things, take the time to do a good job. The pies and pizzas will be worth it.

Some Safety Basics

DECIDING WHERE TO COOK

1. *Be Outside.* Hot charcoal gives off poisonous fumes that are dangerous, even in a fireplace, inside.

2. Look for bare dirt, concrete, or asphalt. Heat can damage grass or wooden decks.

USING THE OVEN

1. Never touch anything but the outside of the oven with your bare hands. Remember that burning charcoal is much hotter than it looks, and the cooked food will be hot too. Use tongs for the charcoal and potholders for the food.

2. Stay close to your oven while the food bakes. Someone might walk by and get burned or spoil your recipe.

3. Use your nose. Food should smell good as it bakes. If you smell something burning, check to see what is wrong.

CLEANING UP

1. Using potholders, carefully fold the foil from under your oven into a bundle, with all the ashes and charcoal inside. Put it into a pan or bucket of water and leave it there for at least two hours. *Never* put it into a trash can while it is still hot.

2. Or, if you are absolutely sure no one will come near your cooking spot, leave the foil and charcoal alone until they cool (about two hours). Then fold it all up and throw it away.

Using a Box Oven

You will need:

a box oven

four 6-ounce *all-metal* juice cans, empty,

> or one soup-sized (about 11 ounces) can,

> empty and with the label torn off

a small rack from a baking pan (optional)

foil

tongs and potholders

hot charcoal (see pages 24–28)

a stick or a pencil

a small pebble

A driveway, patio, concrete porch, or bare ground are all good places to use a box oven. Find a place that is smooth and level and out of the way.

First cover the spot with a sheet or two of foil, shiny side up. The foil helps reflect heat up into the food and keeps the area clean. If it is windy, you might need to put rocks on the corners of the foil.

Next set the four metal cans in a square in

the middle of the foil. They are used to hold up the food, so heat can flow under and all around it. If you have a rack, set it across the tops of the cans. Or, if you are using just one can, set the can in the center of the foil.

Set the oven down over the cans, and carefully draw around it with a pencil or stick. The mark you make on the foil will show you where the box sits.

Remove the box and use tongs to line up hot lumps of charcoal just inside the outline of the box, on all four sides. You will need one briquet for every 40 degrees of temperature. To find out how many briquets to use, divide 40 into the temperature you need. For example, 400 degrees divided by 40 degrees equals 10, so you will use 10 briquets. If the division does not come out even, use one extra briquet.

Now set the box down gently on its outline. None of the charcoal should touch the box. If you aren't sure, lift each side of the box carefully and check. Use the stick to push any briquets that are too close.

Slide the pebble under one edge of the oven to lift it slightly off the ground. Charcoal *must have* some fresh air to be able to burn.

setting up the oven

Let the oven heat for two or three minutes. Then lift it gently and set it down nearby while you get the food.

Set the food you want to bake on top of the rack or the cans. If you are using just one can, be sure to balance the food carefully. Put the oven and the pebble back, and you are ready to bake.

About the same amount of time is needed to bake something in a box oven as in a regular oven. If the recipe calls for twenty minutes, wait twenty minutes before you peek. Sometimes, as in any oven, the food is not quite done when the time is up. If so, put the oven and pebble back and give it a little longer.

If the weather is very cold or windy, a box oven needs special help. Lay a blanket or a sleeping bag over the oven, to keep in the heat. But be careful not to tip the oven, and make sure the blanket does not block the air opening next to the pebble.

If your recipe takes longer than forty-five minutes, you will need to add more hot charcoal. Start the new charcoal heating when you begin baking, and it will be ready when you need it. Just lift the box and use the tongs to line up the fresh charcoal. Don't take the old charcoal out.

A box oven works every time, and it can cook any food you would bake in an oven at home.

The recipes in this section will give you some ideas. Try a few, to be sure you know what to do. Then the next time your scout troop picks a bucket of berries, you will be ready to turn them into a hot berry pie.

Starting Charcoal

Charcoal burns clean and hot, but it is not as easy to light as a campfire. There are many different ways to get it started. All of them take about half an hour, so plan to light your charcoal first. It can be heating while you get the food ready to bake.

THREE WAYS TO LIGHT CHARCOAL:

1. *Use a fire starter*
   and a charcoal chimney

You can buy fire starters at camping supply stores, but it is more fun to make your own. Fill the twelve cups of a cardboard egg carton with sawdust or tiny shreds of newspaper. Ask an adult to melt some old candles or paraffin and pour the wax over the carton. When the wax cools, break off a section to light your fire. This method makes twelve fire starters at a time.

Or you can tear off half a page of newspaper. With your knife, shave wax strips from an old candle and pile a small handful of them on the newspaper. Fold the newspaper into a loose ball and use it to start your fire. This method makes one fire starter.

To construct a charcoal chimney, cut both ends out of an old one-pound coffee can or a large juice can. Ask an adult to help you make air holes all around one end with a drink can opener. Put on gloves and bend back the sharp metal.

To light the charcoal, place a fire starter on a piece of foil and light it with a wooden match. Set the chimney over it, with the air holes at the bottom, and fill the chimney with charcoal.

White smoke will show the charcoal is heating. Leave the chimney alone for about thirty minutes, until the top briquets turn white. Use tongs to lift off the chimney, and the charcoal is ready to use.

You can use the same chimney over and over. But be careful while it is hot.

charcoal chimney

2. *Use self-lighting charcoal*

Some special charcoal will start with a match. Just pile it up and light it, as the instructions say. Or use the charcoal chimney. The charcoal will get hot in about twenty-five minutes.

3. *Have an adult light it*
   with charcoal lighter

This way to start charcoal is the most dangerous. Charcoal lighter can explode if it is not used carefully. This method also takes about half an hour.

Whatever method you use, remember to be careful. Burning charcoal is *hot*.

Recipes for a Box Oven

DESSERTS

Crazy Cake
Easy Oatmeal Squares
Baked Apples
Blueberry Pie
    Easy Blueberry Pie
Peanut Chip Cookies

BREADS

Corn bread
Biscuits
Granola (cereal)
Beer Bread
Oatmeal Yeast Bread

MAIN DISHES

Oven-Fried Chicken
Meat Loaf Muffins
Pizza
    Easy Pizza

VEGETABLES

French Fries
Soupy Green Beans
Baked Beans

CRAZY CAKE

Heat box oven to 350°

1½ cups flour
1 cup sugar
3 tablespoons cocoa
1 teaspoon baking soda
½ teaspoon salt
1 teaspoon vanilla
1 tablespoon vinegar
6 tablespoons cooking oil or melted margarine
1 cup water

      measuring cup
      measuring spoons
      9″ cake pan, round or square
      fork

1. Put all the dry ingredients into the pan, and mix them with the fork.

2. Stir in vanilla, vinegar, and oil.

3. Add water and stir until the batter is smooth. (Be careful to stir into the corners if your pan is square.)

4. Put the batter into the box oven and bake for 25 minutes.

Note: Any cake mix also works well. Just follow directions for time and temperature.

EASY OATMEAL SQUARES

Makes 30 2-inch squares
Heat box oven to 350°

½ cup brown sugar, firmly packed
½ cup sugar
½ cup evaporated milk
1½ cup oatmeal, uncooked
1 6-ounce package chocolate chips
1 6-ounce package butterscotch chips
1 cup nuts, broken into small pieces
½ cup raisins

> 9″ × 13″ baking pan
> margarine, Pam,
>   or any nonstick vegetable spray
> can opener
> measuring cup
> mixing bowl
> large spoon

1. Grease the inside of the pan, or spray with Pam.

2. Mix both sugars and the milk in the bowl. Stir until the sugar dissolves.

3. Mix in the oatmeal.

4. Mix in the chips, nuts, and raisins.

5. Put the mixture into the pan, and pat it

down with clean, greased fingers or the back of a greased spoon.

6. Put the pan into the box oven and bake for 35 minutes.

7. After baking, let the cookies cool for half an hour and then cut them into 30 2-inch squares. (If you cut them too soon, they will fall apart.)

BAKED APPLES

Serves **6**

Heat box oven to 400°

¾ cup brown sugar

1 teaspoon cinnamon

6 firm apples

3 tablespoons butter or margarine

water

milk or cream

> spoon
> measuring cup
> measuring spoons
> small knife
> apple corer
> baking pan

1. Stir the cinnamon into the sugar in the measuring cup.

2. Slice the top from each apple, and carefully cut out the core. Try not to break through at the bottom.

3. Fill each apple with the sugar mixture.

4. Put half a tablespoon of butter on each apple and replace the top.

5. Set the apples in a baking pan, and add enough water to cover the bottom of the pan.

6. Bake for 45 minutes without checking.

(If you move the box and let heat out, you will need to add more charcoal. The apples don't need checking because it is almost impossible to burn baked apples.)

7. Serve hot or cold, with milk or cream.

BLUEBERRY PIE

Serves 6–8
Heat box oven to 425°

CRUST:
2 cups flour
1 teaspoon salt
½ teaspoon baking powder
¾ cup shortening
¼ cup cold milk
1 tablespoon milk
1 teaspoon sugar
FILLING:
4 cups blueberries, fresh or frozen
1 cup sugar
⅓ cup flour
½ teaspoon cinnamon
2 tablespoons margarine or butter
        measuring cup
        measuring spoons
        2 mixing bowls
        spoon
        fork
        strips of foil or countertop, floured
        rolling pin
        knife

9″ pie plate

Pam or other cooking spray

1. Wash and remove stems from fresh blueberries or thaw frozen ones. Set them aside while you make the crust.

2. Mix the flour, salt, and baking powder together in a bowl.

3. Add the shortening and mix it into the flour with a fork until all the lumps are too small to see. The texture should be like cornmeal.

4. Add ¼ cup milk and stir the dough into a ball.

5. Scrape the dough onto some lightly floured foil or a countertop and with clean hands, divide the dough in half. Set one lump aside. Pat the other lump gently into a circle.

6. Use the rolling pin, lightly floured, to flatten the dough into a smooth, thin circle about one inch bigger than the pie plate all around. Use the knife to cut off any ragged edges.

7. Spray the inside of the pie plate with Pam.

8. Fold the circle of dough in half, and lift it carefully onto the plate. Unfold it. If it tears, pat it together with your fingers.

9. Put the blueberries into a bowl and sprinkle on sugar, flour, and cinnamon.

10. Pour the berry mixture into the piecrust.

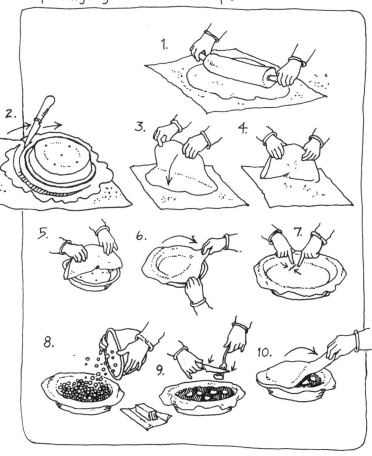

Use the fork to dot little pieces of margarine or butter all over the top.

11. Roll the rest of the dough into a circle just big enough to cover the plate.

12. Fold the top crust over, lay it on top of

the pie, and unfold it. Be careful, because it is not so easy to patch the top.

13. Using a finger and thumb on one hand and the thumb on the other, pinch the top and bottom crust together all around. Or you can press the edges together with a fork.

14. Use the knife to make several slits in the middle of the top crust to let the steam out. You can space them into a design, if you like.

15. Pour one tablespoon milk over the top, and spread it around with your fingers.

16. Sprinkle one teaspoon sugar over the milk.

17. Put the pie into a hot box oven. Bake for 40 minutes, or until the juice bubbles through the slits and the crust is brown on top.

18. Serve warm or cold.

EASY BLUEBERRY PIE

Serves 6–8

Heat box oven to 425°

2 frozen piecrusts, thawed

1 10-ounce box frozen blueberries, thawed,
   or 1 or 2 cups fresh blueberries

1 can blueberry pie filling

1 tablespoon butter or margarine

1 tablespoon milk

1 teaspoon sugar

     measuring cup

     can opener

     spoon

     knife

1. Pour the blueberries into one piecrust.

2. Spread pie filling over the berries and stir gently.

3. Dot tiny pieces of margarine or butter all over the filling.

4. Carefully turn the second piecrust upside down on top of the pie to make a top crust. Smooth it with your fingers. Start from step 13, above, and finish the pie.

PEANUT-CHIP COOKIES

Makes 3–4 dozen
Heat box oven to 375°

½ cup soft butter or margarine
½ cup brown sugar, firmly packed
½ cup sugar
1 egg
½ teaspoon vanilla
¾ cup wheat germ
¾ cup flour
1 teaspoon baking powder
½ teaspoon salt
¼ cup coconut
½ cup unsalted peanuts,
   with brown, papery husks removed
1 6-ounce bag chocolate chips
         measuring cup
         measuring spoons
         mixing bowl
         spoon
         2 cookie sheets
         Pam or other cooking spray
            or extra butter to grease pans
         pancake turner

1. Mix the butter and the sugars together until smooth.

2. Stir in the egg and the vanilla.

3. Stir in all the other ingredients, one or two at a time.

4. Grease or spray the cookie sheet and drop spoonfuls of dough on it, one inch apart.

Note: To keep cookies from burning on the bottom, place the cookie sheet on a tall can. Use your charcoal chimney, or look for a tall juice can or a coffee can.

5. Bake each batch of cookies for about 15 minutes. They will be brown around the edges and soft on top.

6. While the first batch is baking, get a second sheet ready. You can use the same charcoal. But if you need to bake a third batch, add some fresh, hot charcoal.

7. When the cookies cool slightly, remove them from the sheet with a pancake turner.

CORN BREAD

Serves 6–8

Heat box oven to 450°

1¼ cups yellow cornmeal

¼ cup flour

2 tablespoons sugar

1 tablespoon baking powder

1 teaspoon salt

1 egg

1⅛ cup milk

3 tablespoons cooking oil or melted butter

     9″ × 9″ baking pan

     Pam or other cooking spray

       or extra butter to grease pan

     measuring cup

     measuring spoons

     mixing bowl

     spoon

1. Carefully grease the whole inside of the pan.

2. In the mixing bowl, mix together all the dry ingredients.

3. Add the egg, milk, and oil, and stir just until the batter is smooth.

4. Pour the batter into the pan, and bake for

20 minutes. The corn bread should be light brown on top. If it isn't done, bake 5 to 10 minutes longer.

    5. Serve hot.

BISCUITS

Serves 6–8

Heat box oven to 450°

2 cups flour

3 teaspoons baking powder

1 teaspoon salt

½ cup soft margarine or butter

¾ cup milk

honey butter (see step 11 below)

      measuring cup

      measuring spoons

      mixing bowl

      fork

      strip of foil or countertop, floured

      extra flour

      rolling pin

      biscuit cutter or small metal juice can

      9″ × 13″ baking pan

1. Mix all the dry ingredients in the bowl.

2. Put ¼ cup butter in the pan and melt it as you preheat the box oven.

3. Add the other ¼ cup butter to the flour mixture. Use the fork to mix it into the flour. Mix until all the lumps are too small to see.

4. Slowly stir in the milk to make a soft dough.

5. Scrape the dough out onto a floured strip of foil or countertop and, with clean hands, pat it into a flat lump.

6. Fold the dough in half and pat it flat again. Turn the dough and fold it again. Fold and flatten it about ten times, sprinkling it with flour if it seems sticky, until the dough feels smooth.

7. Using a floured rolling pin or your hands, flatten the dough into a smooth sheet about the thickness of your thumb.

8. Cut out round biscuits with the cutter or the can. Refold and use the leftover dough.

9. Dip each biscuit in melted butter and place it, buttered side up, in the pan.

10. Bake for 12 to 15 minutes. The biscuits will be brown on top.

11. Serve hot with honey butter, made by mixing equal parts of soft butter and honey until they are smooth.

GRANOLA

Serves 12

Heat box oven to 270°

3 cups rolled oats
½ cup wheat germ
½ cup chopped walnuts
½ cup sliced almonds
⅔ cup sweetened coconut
⅓ cup brown sugar
½ teaspoon salt
1 teaspoon vanilla
½ cup cooking oil
½ cup raisins
milk or cream

measuring cup
measuring spoons
9″ × 13″ baking pan
fork

1. Mix all the ingredients but the last three together in the pan.

2. Drizzle the oil over the mixture and stir it in.

3. Bake for 45 minutes without checking.

4. Remove the pan from the oven and stir in the raisins.

5. Serve with milk or cream. Extra cereal can be saved to eat later.

BEER BREAD

Serves 6–8

Heat box oven to 350°

3 cups flour

1½ tablespoons baking powder

3 tablespoons sugar

1½ teaspoons salt

1 12-ounce can cold beer

butter or margarine

measuring cup

measuring spoons

mixing bowl

spoon

8″ × 4″ bread pan

Pam or other cooking spray

or margarine to grease pan

1. Stir all the dry ingredients together in the bowl.

2. Add the beer and mix until all the flour is absorbed.

3. Spread the batter into a greased bread pan.

4. Put the pan into a heated box oven.

5. Start a new batch of charcoal heating.

6. After 30 minutes, lift the oven and add fresh, hot charcoal. Do not take out the old charcoal.

7. Bake another 30 minutes, or until the bread is brown and sounds hollow when you thump it with a fingernail.

8. Cool the bread about 10 minutes before cutting it.

9. Serve warm or cold, with butter or margarine.

OATMEAL YEAST BREAD

Makes 2 loaves
Bake at 350°
(Needs two box ovens,
but do not start charcoal yet)

1½ cups very warm water
¼ cup sugar
1 cup rolled oats
1 package dry yeast
2 teaspoons salt
2 egg yolks
⅓ cup cooking oil
1 cup powdered milk
4 cups flour

       measuring cup
       measuring spoon
       mixing bowl
       mixing spoon
       dish towel
       large piece of foil or countertop, floured
       2 8″×4″ bread pans
       butter or margarine to grease pans
       2 shallow metal pans
         (cake pans or mess-kit skillets will do)

1. Pour the water, sugar, and oatmeal into a bowl.

2. Sprinkle the yeast on the mixture, and wait 10 minutes. Do not stir.

3. Stir in everything but the flour.

4. Stir in the flour, one cup at a time, until it is all absorbed. The dough will be lumpy.

5. Cover the bowl with the towel and set it in a warm place for 30 minutes.

6. Stir the dough again, and put it back to rise another 30 minutes.

7. Scrape the dough out onto a large piece of floured foil or a floured countertop.

8. Divide the dough in half. With clean hands, pat each half into a flat square. Fold two sides in toward the middle. Flatten the dough with your hands, and fold the other two sides in toward the middle. Shape the lump gently, smooth side up, into a greased bread pan.

9. Let both loaves rise, covered with the towel, in a warm place for about 1 hour.

10. After the dough has been rising for about 30 minutes, start enough charcoal to heat two box ovens to 350°. Do not preheat the ovens.

11. Set a flat pan of hot water on the ground inside each oven. It does not matter if your can or cans sit inside the pan of water.

12. Put in the charcoal and the bread. Bake

for 40 to 45 minutes, without checking. You will begin to smell the bread as it bakes.

13. When it is done, the bread will be brown and it will sound hollow when you tap it with a fingernail.

14. Remove the bread from the pan and let it cool before you slice it.

OVEN-FRIED CHICKEN

Serves 6

Heat box oven to 425°

12 chicken legs or whatever parts you prefer

½ cup margarine

¼ cup flour

1 cup crushed bran flakes

  or any other unsugared cereal

½ teaspoon salt

        knife

        9″ × 13″ baking pan

        measuring cup

        measuring spoon

        paper lunch bag or plastic bag

1. Cut the stick of margarine into pieces in the pan, and put it into the oven to melt as soon as the charcoal is hot. (Or melt it over another fire.)

2. Mix the flour, crushed cereal, and salt in the bag.

3. Dip each piece of chicken into melted margarine and drop it into the bag. Hold the top closed and shake to coat each piece with the flour mixture.

4. Arrange all the coated chicken pieces in the pan.

5. Bake for 45 to 50 minutes. Add a few pieces of new, hot charcoal after about 30 minutes. (Start the new charcoal heating when you put the chicken in to bake.)

6. Serve hot.

MEAT-LOAF MUFFINS

Serves 6

Heat box oven to 350°
(May require two ovens)

⅔ cup flavored cracker crumbs
1 cup milk
2 eggs
½ cup chopped onion
1 teaspoon salt
¼ teaspoon pepper
1½ pounds lean ground beef
catsup

measuring cup
measuring spoons
mixing bowl
mixing spoon
2 6-cup muffin pans
paper towels

Note: If your oven is too small for two muffin pans, you will need two ovens. Check before you start.

1. Put the cracker crumbs and milk into the bowl. Soak for ten minutes.

2. Stir in eggs, onions, salt, and pepper.

3. Add the meat. Mix well.

4. Pack the meat mixture lightly into the muffin cups.

5. Balance the muffin pans carefully on cans or on a rack inside a heated box oven or ovens.

6. Bake for 40 minutes.

7. Remove the muffins from the pans, and drain them on a plate covered with paper towels.

8. Serve hot with catsup.

PIZZA

Makes 2 large pizzas or 3 small ones
Bake at 400°
(Needs 2 or 3 box ovens,
but do not start charcoal yet)

1 cup whole-wheat flour
1 package active dry yeast
1 teaspoon salt
1 cup very warm water
2 tablespoons cooking oil
2 cups all-purpose flour
1 15-ounce can tomato sauce
½ cup catsup
1 teaspoon oregano
1 tablespoon grated Parmesan cheese
1 cup cooked sausage, hamburger, pepperoni,
   or whatever topping you like on pizza
2 cups grated mozzarella cheese
              measuring cup
              measuring spoons
              2 large mixing bowls
              large spoon
              large piece of foil or pastry cloth
                 or clean countertop
              extra flour
              extra warm water

butter or margarine for greasing

can opener

2 or 3 pizza pans or cookie sheets

1. Mix the whole-wheat flour, the yeast, and the salt together in a bowl.

2. Add the water (as warm as a very hot bath), and stir.

3. Add the oil and stir until the batter is smooth.

4. Stir in the white flour. The batter will be stiff, but it does not have to be smooth. Don't worry if all the flour doesn't mix in.

5. Spread a handful of flour on your large piece of foil or pastry cloth or clean countertop. Scrape out all the dough and leftover flour on top of it.

6. Fill the bowl with warm water, to clean and heat it.

7. With both hands, knead the dough until it is smooth. It takes about five minutes. If you don't know how to knead, here are instructions.

Use your palms, not your fingers. Push down hard on the dough, to flatten it. (Stand on a stool, if you need to, so that you can lean down as you push.) Then fold the dough in half. Push down hard again. Fold it over again. Keep pushing and folding and turning the

kneading dough

1.

2.

3.

4.

5.

6.

raising and spreading dough

1.

2.

3.

4.

5.

6.

7.

8.

dough until it starts to get smooth all over. You will need to sprinkle on more flour if it gets sticky.

8. When the dough is smooth, let it rest for a minute.

9. Clean and dry the bowl and grease the inside.

10. Put the pizza dough into the warm, greased bowl to grease the bottom. Then turn the dough over to grease the top.

11. Cover the bowl with a cloth and leave it in a warm place, for about 45 minutes, to rise. The lump of dough will get twice as big.

12. While the dough is rising, start the charcoal for the box oven. This recipe will make two large pizzas or three small ones. If you want to bake them all at the same time, get two or three ovens ready.

13. Mix together the tomato sauce, the catsup, the oregano, and the tablespoon of Parmesan cheese.

14. Grease two or three pizza pans. (If you want to make only one pizza now, put the rest of the dough and sauce into the refrigerator to use later.)

15. When the dough has doubled in size, use your fist to punch it down. Divide it into two or three pieces, depending on how many pizzas you plan to make.

16. Flatten each piece of dough onto a greased pan. Work from the center and spread it as thin as you can. If holes appear, pinch the edges together.

17. Spread sauce on each pizza.

18. Put on the topping. You can use as many different kinds as you like.

19. Cover each pizza with grated mozzarella cheese.

20. Bake 20 to 25 minutes, until the edges are brown and the cheese is melted. Make sure charcoal is not directly under the edges of the pizza, or it may burn.

Note: Frozen pizzas also work well in a box oven. Just thaw and follow directions.

EASY PIZZA

Serves 12

Heat box oven to 425°

1 15-ounce can tomato sauce
½ cup catsup
½ teaspoon oregano
12 English muffins, split in half
1 pound cooked sausage
½ pound sliced pepperoni
1 can crushed pineapple, drained,
   or whatever you like on pizza
8 ounces mozzarella cheese, grated
8 ounces cheddar cheese, grated
      can opener
      measuring cup
      measuring spoon
      small mixing bowl
      several large spoons
      2 pizza pans or cookie sheets

1. Mix together the tomato sauce, catsup, and oregano in a bowl.

2. Place the muffin halves on the pans, split side up.

3. Top each muffin half with a big spoonful of sauce.

4. Then add sausage, pepperoni, and pine-apple, or whatever you like to each.

5. Mix the cheeses together and put a big spoonful on each.

6. Put the first pan of pizzas into a hot box oven and bake for 20 minutes, until the cheese is melted and the muffin is slightly browned.

7. You can use the same charcoal to bake the second batch or use two ovens.

FRENCH FRIES

Serves 6

Heat box oven to 500°

2 teaspoons cooking oil

½ small bag frozen French fries, thawed

salt

    measuring spoon

    1 pizza pan or baking sheet

1. Pour the oil onto the pan.

2. Spread the French fries in a single layer on the pan. Stir gently to coat them with oil.

3. Bake for 25 minutes.

4. Salt and serve hot.

SOUPY GREEN BEANS

Serves 6

Heat box oven to 350°

1 can cream of chicken soup
  (or cream of celery or mushroom)
1 small package frozen green beans
½ soup can water
¼ cup sunflower seeds

        can opener
        baking pan
        spoon
        measuring cup

1. Mix soup, beans, and water in the pan.
2. Spread the seeds on top.
3. Bake for 20 minutes.

BAKED BEANS

Serves 6

Heat box oven to 400°

1 medium can baked beans (about 21 ounces)

¼ cup catsup

3 tablespoons molasses

1 tablespoon chopped onion

1 strip bacon, cut in half

      can opener

      measuring cup

      measuring spoon

      knife

      baking dish with lid

1. Mix all the ingredients in the dish.

2. Cover and bake for 20 minutes.

COOKING ON A CAN

Cooking out-of-doors is most often done over a campfire, but this can be the hardest way to cook. Unlike your kitchen stove, campfires don't have burners to set the pans on, and they are hard to control. Sometimes the fires are so hot they burn the bacon, and then they go out just as you are ready to put in the eggs. A tin-can stove, however, can make it easy for everyone to be his or her own cook. A large can is the stove top, and a small can underneath holds the heat.

The next few pages will tell you how to make a tin-can stove and use it safely. If you are cooking in a group, everyone might like to make his or her own stove. Or you can work in pairs. A tin-can stove cooks best for one or two people at a time.

Tin-can stoves are especially good for breakfast. Bacon and eggs are one of the easiest meals to cook on them. Pancakes are harder, so try a few of the other things first. This book gives recipes for breakfasts and for main dishes, vegetables, soups, drinks, and snacks. After you learn how to use a tin-can stove, you can fix your own favorite foods.

Some foods can be cooked right on top of the can. Others need a skillet or a pan. Girl or Boy Scout mess-kit pans are perfect, but any small metal pans will do.

With a tin-can stove, you don't always have to start with one thing at a time. Bacon helps grease the stove for pancakes or eggs. Your soup can be steeping while your sandwich cooks. Just look over the recipes and decide how much you want to try at once.

Making a Tin-Can Stove

You will need:
a large tin can (3-pound coffee cans work best,
      but a 2-pound coffee can
      or large fruit juice can will do)
tin snips
gloves
a punch-type can opener

A tin-can stove is made from a large tin

can, open at one end. The bottom of the can is
the top of your stove.

First tear off the paper on the outside of the
can, if there is any, and make sure the bottom
of the can is clean. If it is rusted, find another
can.

The stove needs air holes near the top. Hook
the can opener over the rim of the closed end,
pointing down, so that it makes holes in the side
of the can instead of the top. Make four holes,
evenly spaced around the can.

The next step is to make a door, for air and

tin-can stove

for tending the fire. You may want to ask an adult to help with this part. Wearing gloves, use the tin snips to cut two slits in the can, about three inches high and three inches apart. Still wearing gloves, fold back the metal between the slits, to make an open doorway. Fold the metal back as far as you can so that it will be out of the way. (Be careful. The edges are sharp.)

A tin-can stove can be used over and over, if you keep its top clean and dry. The bigger the can, the more stove you have to work with.

Heating a Tin-Can Stove

You will need:
a clean 7½-ounce tuna-fish can
        (or other can that size)
strips of corrugated cardboard
        (grocery cartons are made
        of corrugated cardboard)
melted paraffin or candle wax
aluminum foil

You can heat your tin-can stove in several

ways. You can put hot charcoal under it or even build a tiny campfire inside. The easiest way, however, is to use a buddy burner.

Buddy burners are simple to make. Cut corrugated cardboard into strips that are just a lit-

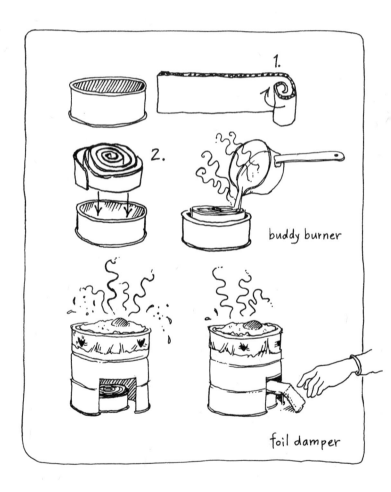

buddy burner

foil damper

tle wider than a tuna-fish can is tall. Roll the strips loosely until you have a roll almost as big as the inside of the can. Put the roll in the can, and let it unwind until it fills it. Don't pack the cardboard in tightly, or there won't be room for air.

Ask an adult to pour melted wax into the can until it is almost full. It will hold about one-eighth to one-quarter of a pound. Let the wax cool.

Sometimes buddy burners burn too hot, and you want to "turn down" the fire. Fold a sheet of foil about two feet long in half three times. You will have a strip about as wide as the door to your tin-can stove. Fold the strip a little smaller, if you need to, to make sure it fits through the door. Then slide it in and use it as a damper to cover part of the fire if the stove gets too hot.

Some Safety Basics

DECIDING WHERE TO COOK

1. *Be outside.* Burning paraffin makes poisonous fumes.

2. Look for the same kind of place you would use for a box oven (see page 20). If you are part of a group, leave plenty of space between cans, so no one will bump someone else's stove.

USING THE STOVE

1. Tin-can stoves are hot on top and *all the way down the sides.* Never touch any part of the stove with your bare hands or knees as you work. Wear jeans or other sturdy pants, just in case.

2. Have a box of salt handy. There is no reason for a buddy burner to tip over while it is on fire. But if one did, salt is the best way to put out a spilled paraffin fire. *Never* use water. Water can make the fire spread.

CLEANING UP

1. Wad up a paper towel and wipe off any grease.

2. Using two potholders, pick up the stove with both hands. Turn it over and set it down

on top of the buddy burner to smother the fire. Leave it about an hour, until everything cools.

Using a Tin-Can Stove

You will need:
aluminum foil
a tin-can stove and buddy burner
Pam or any nonstick vegetable spray (optional)
wooden matches
two potholders

Most foods can be cooked right on top of the stove, but it will stay cleaner if you cover the top with foil. Tear a piece of foil a little bigger than the stove top, and smooth it down over the top and sides. If it covers the air holes, poke through the foil with a stick to clear them.

Find a safe, level place to set your buddy burner, and light it with a wooden match. You may need to tip the can sideways to get the cardboard to catch fire. You may safely tip it with your hand at this stage, but don't touch the can after it starts to burn.

Spray the stove top or the foil covering with Pam, if you like, and set the stove over the fire. It will be hot enough to cook on almost immediately.

Follow the recipe for whatever you want to cook. If the fire is too hot, insert the folded foil damper through the door, to slow it down. If the stove is not hot enough, check to see if the fire needs relighting.

Sometimes a buddy burner runs out of wax while you are cooking. If it keeps going out, relight the cardboard and put in a piece of candle. Adding new wax will keep the buddy burner burning for hours.

When you are through eating and everything has cooled (see pages 74–75), turn the stove upside down and store the buddy burner inside. Clean and dry the top, but don't try to remove the black inside the stove. Put the whole thing away for next time.

Recipes for a Tin-Can Stove

BREAKFASTS	Egg-in-a-Hole
	Bacon and Eggs
	Hot Applesauce and Granola
	French Toast
	Pancakes
MAIN DISHES	Hamburger
	Hawaiian Ham Sandwiches
SOUPS AND DRINKS	Egg Drop Soup
	Vegetable Soup
	Cocoa
	Hot Spiced Cider
VEGETABLES	Corn and Tomatoes
	Candied Carrots
SNACKS	Fudge

EGG-IN-A-HOLE

Serves 1
1 slice of bread
margarine or butter
1 egg
salt
pepper
pancake turner

1. Tear an egg-sized hole in the middle of the bread.

2. Grease the top of a hot tin-can stove with margarine. The easiest way is to tear the paper from one end of a stick of margarine and rub the stick on the stove.

3. Lay your bread on the stove, and break an egg into the hole.

4. Cook until the egg begins to harden on the bottom and the bread turns brown underneath. Use the pancake turner to check.

5. Insert turner under the bread and egg, rub a little more margarine onto the stove, and carefully turn the bread over.

6. Cook for another minute or two, until the egg is done the way you like it. Add salt and pepper to taste.

7. Remove the egg-in-a-hole and eat it on a plate or with your fingers.

BACON AND EGGS

Serves 1

1 or 2 pieces of bacon

1 egg

2 teaspoons milk or water
   (if you want to scramble egg)

salt

pepper

> knife
> fork
> paper towels
> cup or bowl
> measuring spoon
> pancake turner

1. Cut the bacon in half, and lay the pieces on a hot tin-can stove.

2. Use the fork to turn the bacon once or twice as it fries.

3. When the bacon is crisp, lay it on a paper towel.

4. Blot up any puddles of bacon grease with a wadded paper towel. Use the towel to spread the grease all over the stove top, so the egg won't stick.

If you want a fried egg:

5. Break your egg onto the stove. Add salt and pepper.

6. When the bottom is cooked, use the turner to flip the egg over.

If you want a scrambled egg:

5. With a fork, beat the egg, milk, and a sprinkle of salt and pepper together in the cup or bowl.

6. Pour the egg mixture onto the stove.

7. With the fork, gently scrape it from the edges toward the center as it cooks.

8. When the egg is cooked the way you like it, use the turner to lift it off the stove.

HOT APPLESAUCE AND GRANOLA

Serves 2

1 cup applesauce
1 cup granola
milk or cream

measuring cup
small pan
spoon

1. Heat the applesauce in the pan, stirring carefully so that it does not burn on the bottom. Use your damper to keep the fire from getting too hot.

2. When the applesauce is hot, remove it from the stove and stir in the granola.

3. Pour into two dishes, and eat it with milk or cream.

FRENCH TOAST

Serves 2

3 eggs

½ cup milk

1 tablespoon sugar

1 dash salt

margarine or butter

4 slices bread

syrup, jam, or powdered sugar

      measuring cup

      measuring spoon

      mixing bowl

      fork

      pancake turner

1. Beat eggs, milk, sugar, and salt together with a fork.

2. Grease the top of a hot tin-can stove with margarine.

3. Dip both sides of a piece of bread in the egg mixture, and lay it on the stove. Be careful that the fire is not too hot. You may need to use the damper.

4. When the bottom browns, turn the toast over with a fork or the turner. You may need more margarine.

5. When the second side is brown, remove the toast to a plate and eat it with margarine and your favorite topping while another slice cooks.

PANCAKES

Serves 6

¼ cup margarine, melted, or cooking oil
2 eggs
2 cups milk
1 tablespoon sugar
1 teaspoon salt
2 cups flour
5 teaspoons baking powder
extra margarine or butter
syrup or jam

Pam or other cooking spray
small pan
  or aluminum foil shaped into a cup
measuring cup
measuring spoon
mixing bowl
fork
mixing spoon
pancake turner

1. Before heating the stove, spray it with Pam.

2. Put ¼ cup margarine in the pan, and set it on the stove to melt. Or use oil.

3. Break the eggs into the bowl, and beat them with the fork.

4. Stir in the milk, sugar, salt, and melted shortening.

5. Add the flour and baking powder a little at a time. Stir until most of the lumps are gone.

Note: It is important to get the fire under the tin-can stove just right for pancakes. If it is too hot, they will burn before they cook. If it isn't hot enough, they won't cook at all. Sprinkle a drop or two of water on the stove top. The drops should bounce. Use your damper if the fire is too hot, and add wax if it isn't hot enough.

6. Rub the end of a stick of margarine or butter across the stove top, or rub the top with margarine or butter on a paper towel.

7. Pour on enough batter to cover almost all of the stove top.

8. When the pancake is bubbly all over, gently turn it over with the turner. A fork in the other hand helps hold it steady.

9. Cook the second side about as long as the first. Use the turner to lift an edge and check.

10. Regrease the stove top and cook another pancake. In case a few burn, you can make more.

11. Eat each pancake while it is hot, with butter and syrup or jam.

Note: If you like, use any good pancake mix instead of the recipe.

HAMBURGER

Serves 2

⅓ to ½ pound lean hamburger

2 hamburger buns

catsup, mustard, pickles,
   or whatever you like

      Pam or other cooking spray

      pancake turner

      fork

1. Before you heat the stove, spray the top with Pam.

2. Using clean hands, flatten half the hamburger into a patty.

3. Cook the meat on a hot tin-can stove for about 5 minutes, until the bottom is crisp and brown.

4. Use the turner to turn the meat. A fork in the other hand helps hold it steady.

5. Cook the second side several minutes, until it is done the way you like it.

6. Use the turner to slide the hamburger onto a bun. Serve hot.

7. Cook the second hamburger the same way.

HAWAIIAN HAM SANDWICHES

Serves 2

2 slices boiled ham
2 slices cheese
2 slices pineapple
2 hamburger buns

Pam or other cooking spray
pancake turner

1. Before you heat the stove, spray the top with Pam.

2. Lay a slice of ham on a hot tin-can stove.

3. Lay a slice of cheese on top of the ham.

4. Lay a slice of pineapple on top of the cheese.

5. When the cheese begins to melt, slide the turner under the ham and lift the whole thing onto a bun. Eat it while it is hot.

6. Cook the second sandwich the same way.

EGG DROP SOUP

Serves 2–3

1 can chicken broth
½ soup can water
dash of salt
1 egg

      can opener
      small pan with lid
      dish or cup
      fork

1. Mix the soup, water, and salt in the pan and put on the lid. Set the pan on a hot tin-can stove. (Let the fire burn as hot as possible.)

2. Break the egg into the dish or cup, and beat it with the fork.

3. When the soup begins to boil, take off the lid.

4. Pour the beaten egg into the boiling soup, and stir vigorously with the fork.

5. Carefully take the soup off the stove with a potholder. Serve hot.

VEGETABLE SOUP

Serves 2

1 can beef or chicken broth
1 soup can water, if needed
1 handful vegetables,
   such as carrots, celery, and/or onions
1 tablespoon Minute Rice, if you like

> can opener
> small pan with lid
> sharp knife
> spoon
> measuring spoon

1. Put the soup in the pan, and cover with the lid. Set it on a hot tin-can stove. (Let the fire burn as hot as possible.)

2. Cut the vegetables into tiny squares or sticks about the size of a matchstick.

3. When the soup comes to a full, bubbling boil, take it off the stove carefully, with a potholder. Set it in a safe place.

4. Put in the vegetables and the rice, and re-cover with the lid.

5. Wait 5 minutes. (You can cook a sandwich while you wait.) The soup is ready when the vegetables are slightly soft.

COCOA

Serves 2

1½ cups milk

3 tablespoons instant cocoa powder
   or 2 squirts liquid instant cocoa

2 marshmallows

      measuring cup

      measuring spoon

      small pan

      small spoon

1. Warm the milk on a tin-can stove. Stir once or twice.

2. Stir in the cocoa.

3. Serve hot with marshmallows.

HOT SPICED CIDER

Serves 2–3

2 cups apple cider
2 sticks cinnamon
2 cloves

measuring cup
small pan with lid
spoon

1. Put all the ingredients in the pan, cover with the lid, and heat.

2. When the cider barely comes to a boil, remove it from the stove.

3. Let the hot cider stand for several minutes.

4. Remove the cinnamon and cloves, and serve the cider hot.

CORN AND TOMATOES

Serves 4–6

1 15-ounce can whole kernel corn

1 8-ounce can tomato sauce

1 teaspoon sugar

1 tablespoon margarine

       can opener

       measuring spoon

       small pan

       spoon

1. Stir all ingredients together in the pan.

2. Heat on a tin-can stove, stirring often, until the mixture just comes to a boil.

3. Serve hot.

CANDIED CARROTS

Serves 2

1 tablespoon butter
1 tablespoon brown sugar
½ cup frozen sliced carrots
    measuring spoon
    small pan
    spoon

1. Melt the butter in sugar in the pan on a hot tin-can stove.

2. Stir in the carrots, and cover with a lid.

3. Cook about 5 minutes or until the carrots are soft. Stir several times.

4. Serve hot.

FUDGE

Serves 6–12

1 cup brown sugar

½ cup margarine

½ cup chocolate chips

¼ cup milk

3 cups powdered sugar

½ cup nuts

> pie plate (or two mess-kit skillets)
> Pam or other cooking spray
> measuring cup
> small pan with lid
> mixing bowl
> mixing spoon

1. Spray the inside of the pan with Pam.

2. Melt brown sugar, margarine, and chocolate chips together in the pan over a not-too-hot tin-can stove. (A used buddy burner or your damper will give you the right heat.) Stir often.

3. When the first three ingredients have melted, stir in the milk.

4. When the milk is blended in, cover the pan. Cook until the mixture is just at the boiling point. Take off the lid and stir several times.

5. When the mixture starts to boil, take it off the stove. Cool for 15 minutes.

6. Measure half the sugar into a mixing bowl.

7. Beat the cooled fudge into the sugar until it is smooth.

8. Beat in the rest of the sugar. Add the nuts.

9. Scrape the fudge into a Pam-sprayed plate or plates. Let it finish cooling.

10. The fudge will be very soft. When it sets, cut it into squares. (If you like it harder, put it into a refrigerator or a cooler.)

TOASTING ON A WIRE

In a kitchen, most cooks toast bread in an electric toaster. If you peek inside, you can see red-hot wires coiled close to the bread, but not touching it. Heat from the wires makes the bread hot and toasty brown, but if the hot wires happen to touch it, they can burn it black.

Over a campfire, the easiest way to toast bread and other foods is with a different kind of toaster. You can make it from two coat hangers, and it doesn't need any electricity. The next few pages will tell you how to make and use a wire toaster safely.

The wire toaster cooks one thing at a time, so everyone should make his or her own. Two people can share one, but if you try to share with too many, the first cooks will be through eating before the last ones get their turn.

The easiest things to cook on a wire toaster are bread and simple sandwiches. The hardest things are hamburgers, because you have to cook in foil and you can't see what you are doing, and fish, because it takes a long time.

The best reason for cooking in a wire toaster is that you will not make any mess or dirty any pans or dishes. You can use it camping, at the park, or even in the fireplace at home, and it is a handy tool to have in places where you are not allowed to cut green sticks. Besides, you can cook more things in a wire toaster than you can on a stick, and it won't make holes in the food.

Try a piece of toast, first, for breakfast. When you learn how to toast bread just the way you like it, you will be ready to try one of the other recipes in this section and toast your lunch or dinner.

Making a Wire Toaster

You will need:
two wire coat hangers, unpainted
3 inches of thin wire,
    such as picture-hanging wire
½ sheet of newspaper
masking or plastic tape (not Scotch tape)
wire cutters
gloves

Ask an adult to cut the hook off both hangers, right below the twisted part. Straighten each wire into a long rod.

Using gloves, take hold of the rod with both hands, about one-third of the way from one end, and make a right-angle bend (see the picture).

About two and one-half inches up from the bend, make another bend. It doesn't matter if your corners are somewhat round. Make three more bends, keeping the wire as flat as you can.

Bend the other coat hanger the same way. Make them as alike as you can and as flat as possible. Lay each one on a table or other flat place to check. Smooth out the whole wire with your fingers.

Now put one wire on top of the other, with the bent ends pointing in the same direction. Fasten them together at the straight end by winding tape around and around them for about six inches. Cover the sharp ends with tape.

When metal wires get hot, heat travels all the way to the ends. To make a heat-proof handle, fold the newspaper and wrap it around the taped part of the wire. Cover the paper with more tape. Make it tight and smooth so the handle won't slip and will feel comfortable in your hand.

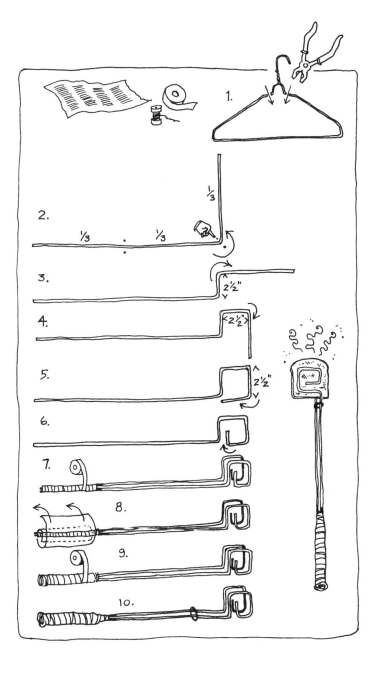

1.

2. $\frac{1}{3}$ $\frac{1}{3}$ $\frac{1}{3}$

3. $2\frac{1}{2}"$

4. $2\frac{1}{2}$

5. $2\frac{1}{2}"$

6.

7.

8.

9.

10.

Now check the other end of the toaster. The bent wires should not be tangled together. If they are, shape them until they stay apart.

Wrap the piece of thin wire in a ring around both coat-hanger wires, right below the first bend. Don't wrap it too tightly, because it has to slide up and down the wires.

When you slide the twisted wire ring down toward the handle, the bent ends of the toaster will come apart so that you can slip food between them. When you slide the ring back up to the bend, it locks the wires together and holds the food in.

Try putting a piece of bread in your toaster. If the bread slips out when the toaster is locked, you need to bend the coat hangers closer together.

A wire toaster will last for years. If the handle gets worn or dirty, just put on a new one.

Some Safety Basics

DECIDING WHERE TO COOK

1. Use any outdoor or indoor fireplace.

2. Cook over charcoal or a wood fire, but be sure the fire has burned down to hot coals and there are no longer any flames.

3. If you are indoors, open the fire screen just enough to put in the toaster. Watch for sparks.

USING THE TOASTER

1. Remember that the whole toaster will get hot, except for the handle.

2. If your food catches fire, *leave it in the fireplace.*

Food that touches a flame can start to burn. If it does, lay the toaster down and wait until the burning stops. Don't try to save your sandwich. When the flames die down, you can try again, over coals.

CLEANING UP

1. Usually a toaster does not need cleaning. If anything sticks, wash the toaster in soapy water and dry it so it won't rust.

Using a Wire Toaster

You will need:

hot charcoal or the embers of a wood fire

potholder

All you have to do is lock food into a wire toaster and hold it over the coals. Find a comfortable place to sit or kneel by the fire so you can keep the toaster level. If you stand up, your food will brown too fast on the end.

When one side cooks, turn the toaster over. Some foods need frequent turning, so the inside gets hot before the outside browns.

The most important thing to remember is to keep the toaster over hot coals, not over flames. Flames will burn the food before it has a chance to cook, so wait until the fire is ready.

Recipes for a Wire Toaster

SANDWICHES   Grilled Cheese or Ham
                   Grilled Tuna
                   Hot Dog
                   Hamburger

TOAST   Toasted Bread, Waffles,
                       and Sweet Rolls
                   Honey Butter
                   Cinnamon Butter
                   Brown Sugar Butter
                   Honey and Peanut Butter

MAIN DISHES   Steak
                   Trout

GRILLED CHEESE or GRILLED HAM SANDWICH

Serves 1

2 slices bread, any kind
soft butter
1 or 2 slices cheese, any kind,
   or 1 or 2 slices boiled ham
      knife

1. Spread both slices of bread lightly with butter.

2. Put the cheese or ham between slices of bread, butter side in.

3. Toast over hot coals until the bread is brown and the cheese is melted or the ham is hot.

Note: For grilled ham and cheese, mix the two.

GRILLED TUNA SANDWICH

Serves 4–6

1 can tuna fish
¼ cup mayonnaise
2 tablespoons sweet pickle relish, if you like
8 or 10 slices bread

> can opener
> small bowl
> fork
> knife

1. Open the can and drain the oil from the tuna fish.

2. In the bowl, mix the mayonnaise and relish and tuna together.

3. Spread the tuna mixture on bread, and cover with another slice of bread.

4. Toast until the bread is brown and the filling is hot.

HOT DOG

Serves 1

1 or 2 hot dogs

1 or 2 hot-dog buns

mustard or catsup

knife

1. Split 1 or 2 hot dogs in half, lengthwise.

2. Fasten them inside the toaster and cook over hot coals.

3. Put 2 halves on each bun, and serve hot with mustard or catsup.

HAMBURGER

Serves 1

⅓ pound hamburger

hamburger bun

salt

pepper

mustard or catsup

aluminum foil

potholder

1. Flatten the meat into a patty, and wrap it in foil, shiny side in.

2. Fasten the foil-wrapped meat in the toaster, and cook over hot coals for about 4 minutes on each side. You will hear the meat sizzle as it cooks.

3. When you think it is done, unwrap it carefully with a potholder. If it needs more cooking, rewrap it and toast a few minutes longer.

4. Put the hamburger on a bun, and serve hot with mustard or catsup and salt and pepper.

BREAKFAST TOAST, WAFFLES, OR SWEET ROLLS

slices of any kind of bread or frozen waffles or
  large, flat sweet rolls
butter or margarine
jam, syrup, or toppings (see recipes below)
  Pam or other cooking spray

1. Spray the toaster with Pam. (This is not necessary for plain bread.)

2. Fasten a slice of bread, a frozen waffle, or a sweet roll in the toaster and toast over hot coals until it is hot and brown.

3. Serve hot with butter and jam or syrup, or with one of the following toppings:

HONEY BUTTER: Mix equal parts of honey and soft butter until smooth.

CINNAMON BUTTER: Mix ¼ cup sugar and 1 teaspoon cinnamon with ½ cup soft butter, and stir until smooth.

BROWN SUGAR BUTTER: Mix ¼ cup brown sugar with ½ cup soft butter, and stir until smooth.

HONEY AND PEANUT BUTTER: Mix equal parts of honey and peanut butter until smooth.

STEAK

Serves 1

1 thin steak (can be almost any kind,
   with or without bone)
tenderizer, if needed
salt
pepper

Pam or other cooking spray
fork

1. Spray the toaster with Pam.

2. If you think the steak needs tenderizing, apply meat tenderizer according to the instructions on the bottle.

3. Fasten the steak in the toaster, and cook over coals about four minutes on each side, or until it is done the way you like it.

4. Serve hot with salt and pepper.

TROUT

Serves 1

1 small trout, cleaned
    (frozen trout should be thawed ahead of time)
salt

pepper

1 strip bacon

    Pam or other cooking spray
    fork

1. Spray the toaster with Pam.

2. Salt and pepper the inside of the fish.

3. Wrap bacon around the outside of the fish, and fasten it in the toaster.

4. Cook, turning often, until the skin becomes brown and crisp and the meat flakes when you poke through the skin with a fork.

FRYING/STEAMING
IN PAPER

Cooking in paper doesn't need any pots or pans or gadgets. There is nothing to make and nothing to wash. You cook and eat right out of a paper bag or off a piece of newspaper.

But cooking in paper is not easy. It takes skill and patience. Paper burns, and if you aren't careful, your breakfast can catch fire. If you are a beginning outdoor cook, try one of the other methods first. When you can fry a perfect pancake on a tin-can stove and brown a sandwich just the way you like it in a wire toaster, you will be ready to try paper-bag cooking.

There are two ways to cook in paper. Food wrapped in wet newspaper will steam, becoming moist and juicy, right on top of the fire. Or you can fold your food into a paper lunch sack and fry it just above the glowing coals.

Quite a few foods can be cooked in paper, but some are easier than others. The next few pages will tell you what works best and how to cook it safely. Steaming in paper needs foods that cook quickly, and frying in a bag needs food with its own fat.

Cooking in paper takes practice, but knowing how is worth the trouble. A person who can fry his or her own bacon and eggs in a bag for breakfast and steam a big fish on the coals for everyone's dinner is a real outdoor cook.

Some Safety Basics

DECIDING WHERE TO COOK

1. Use any indoor or outdoor fireplace.

2. Cook over charcoal or a wood fire, but be sure the fire has burned down to hot coals, with no flames left.

3. If you are indoors, open the fire screen as little as possible.

USING PAPER

1. Remember that dry paper burns if it touches hot coals. Keep the newspaper wet and the paper bag just above the coals.

2. *Never* bring burning food out of the fireplace. If your paper bag begins to burn, the food will be ruined. Drop it in the fire and start over.

3. If food wrapped in wet newspaper begins to burn, squirt out the flames with water and go on cooking. The food will probably be OK.

CLEANING UP

1. Put everything in the fire and burn it, or throw it in the trash when it is cool.

Cooking in Paper

Since this kind of outdoor cooking is the most complicated, each recipe tells you exactly what to do. The most important thing is the fire—hot coals but no flames. The next most important thing is patience. Give the food time to cook.

Good luck. Have fun.

Recipes for Cooking in Paper

IN A PAPER BAG   Bacon and Eggs

IN NEWSPAPER   Trout
Fish Filets
Steamed Clams
Corn on the Cob
Asparagus

BACON AND EGGS

Serves 1
1 strip bacon
1 egg
salt
pepper
     knife
     paper lunch bag
     sturdy stick or fireplace poker
     small fork

1. Cut the bacon in half, and place both halves, side by side, in the bottom of the bag.

2. Break the egg on top of the bacon.

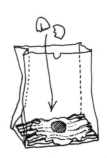

3. Fold the top of the bag over, and make a hole for the stick or poker to fit through.

4. Using the stick or poker, hold the bag over the fire, close to the coals. You will hear the bacon begin to sizzle.

5. Cook until the bacon stops sizzling. It will take about ten minutes. If the egg isn't quite done when you take it off the fire, put it back for a few more minutes.

6. Tear off the top of the bag. Salt and pepper and eat your bacon and eggs, using the bottom of the bag for a plate.

TROUT

Serves 6–12

12 trout, cleaned

   (frozen trout should be thawed ahead of time)

salt

12 slices bacon

   12 full sheets of wet newspaper

   tongs

   a water gun or squirt bottle

   fork

1. Salt the inside of each fish, and wrap a strip of bacon around it.

2. Wrap each fish in a sheet of wet news-

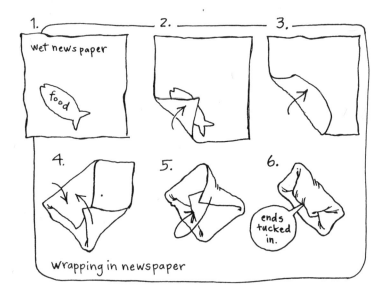

paper, starting at one end and rolling it over and over. Tuck in the loose ends.

3. Using tongs, lay each fish in hot, glowing coals or the hot ashes around them.

4. Cook 15 to 20 minutes, turning the bundles often with the tongs.

5. As the paper dries, squirt it with the water gun. Be careful not to put out the fire. It does not matter if the paper chars or turns black.

6. When the time is up, remove the paper-wrapped fish with tongs and unwrap it on a heat-proof place.

7. Test whether it is done with a fork. The meat should flake easily off the bones. If it isn't done, rewrap the fish in fresh, wet paper and cook longer. Note: The bacon will not cook completely. If you like, you can save it in a cool place and recook it for breakfast.

8. Remove all the trout and serve them hot.

FISH FILETS

Serves 4–6

1 2-pound filet of cod or any other large fish
   or several smaller pieces
salt
2 tablespoons soft margarine or butter
         a strip of waxed paper
         3 full sheets of wet newspaper
         tongs
         water gun or squirt bottle
         fork

1. Salt the fish and spread butter on both sides.

2. Wrap the fish loosely in waxed paper.

3. Lay the waxed-paper-wrapped fish on 3 sheets of wet newspaper, and wrap the fish carefully, tucking in the loose ends.

4. Steam in the coals for 25 to 30 minutes, turning often with tongs. Use the water gun to squirt the paper as it begins to dry or to squirt out the flames if the bundle catches fire. Be careful not to squirt out the fire.

5. When the time is up, remove the bundle to a heat-proof place and carefully unwrap the fish. It should flake when touched with a fork.

6. Serve hot.

STEAMED CLAMS

Serves 1–2

1 dozen steamer clams in their shells

2 tablespoons melted butter

1 tablespoon lemon juice

3 full sheets of wet newspaper

water gun or squirt bottle

tongs

measuring spoon

small fork

1. Wrap the clams in three sheets of wet newspaper, tucking in the loose ends.

2. Using tongs, lay the wet bundle onto a bed of glowing coals.

3. Steam the clams for about 20 minutes, turning often with the tongs. As parts of the paper begin to dry, squirt them with the water gun. It does not matter if the paper turns black and chars in spots.

4. When the time is up, remove the bundle with tongs and unwrap it on a safe place, such as bare dirt or a hearth. The clams should be open and ready to eat. If they have not opened completely, wrap them in fresh wet newspaper and cook them a little longer.

5. Serve hot, with lemon and butter.

CORN ON THE COB

Serves 6–12

12 ears of corn, with the husk still on
butter or margarine
salt

> pan or bucket of water
> 12 full sheets of wet newspaper
> tongs
> water gun or squirt bottle

1. Carefully pull back the husk of each ear of corn, and remove the silk.

2. Wrap the husk back around each ear, and dip the corn into water.

3. Wrap each ear in a sheet of wet newspaper, tucking in the loose ends.

4. Lay the corn in a bed of hot coals.

5. Steam the corn for 15 minutes, turning it often with the tongs. It doesn't matter if the paper turns black and chars, but squirt out any flames.

6. When the time is up, remove the ears with tongs and unwrap them carefully.

7. Serve hot, with butter and salt.

ASPARAGUS

Serves 4–6
12 stalks fresh asparagus
butter or margarine
salt

strip of waxed paper
3 full sheets of wet newspaper
tongs
water gun or squirt bottle

1. Break off the tough bottom end of each stalk of asparagus.

2. Rinse the asparagus and wrap it, dripping wet, loosely in waxed paper.

3. Wrap again, in three sheets of wet newspaper, tucking in the loose ends.

4. Steam in the coals for 15 minutes, turning it often with the tongs. It doesn't matter if the paper turns black and chars, but squirt out any flames.

5. When the time is up, remove the package with tongs and unwrap it carefully. If the asparagus is not as done as you like, rewrap it in fresh wet newspaper and cook 5 to 10 minutes longer.

6. Serve hot with butter and salt.

Index of Recipes